The **BIG** Done Showed **UP!**

Prophetess Patrice Jacques

ROYSTON
Publishing

BK Royston Publishing
P. O. Box 4321
Jeffersonville, IN 47131
502-802-5385
http://www.bkroystonpublishing.com
bkroystonpublishing@gmail.com

© Copyright – 2022

All Rights Reserved. No part of this book may be reproduced, stored in a retrieval system, or transmitted by any means without the written permission of the author.

Cover Photo: Leroy Sanders from New Orleans, LA
Additional editing and proofing: LeNeshia R. Markey, MAT

ISBN-13: 978-1-955063-78-4

King James Version Scriptural Text – Public Domain

Printed in the United States of America

Dedication

This book is dedicated to: The ultimate Creator of my life THE BIG! THE BIG GOD who is creator of all that exist. Thank you, Daddy GOD, for entrusting me with "THE BIG DONE SHOWED UP" Revelation. You Showed Up and Out. I am humbled by this task and will endeavor to bring you All the Glory through it. THE BIG showed Up and has changed my life forever!

To my four outstanding phenomenal children, JaJuan, Zachary Jr., Dana, and Rachael, Mom loves you and I'm so blessed to be chosen by God to have been chosen to be your mother, Thanks for all the love, encouragement and support.

And to my Grandchildren, Lauren Kaya, Kaleb, Calvin, Stormei, Skei and, Santana, and my Great-Grands Isaiah, and Jeremiah, thank you all for loving me, and making my legacy a tailored made sweet one. Grammy love you'll beyond measure.

**Prophetess Patrice Jacques,
"Mama Big"**

THE BIG DONE SHOWED UP!

Acknowledgements

A special thanks to my friends, sisters and brothers and Prophet Frank Delaney for being special friend and pusher!

I am also thankful to my spiritual son and daughters for their love, support and prayers.

THE BIG DONE SHOWED UP!

Table of Contents

Dedication	iii
Acknowledgements	v
Introduction	xi
Day 1 - 2 Corinthians 10:3-6 (KJV)	1
Day 2 - Proverbs 3:5-6 (KJV)	5
Day 3 - Proverbs 23:7 (KJV)	7
Day 4 - Joshua 1:8 (KJV)	9
Day 5 - Deuteronomy 6:6 (KJV)	11
Day 6 - Exodus 3: 17 (KJV)	13
Day 7 - James 1:8 (KJV)	15
Day 8 - Psalm 118:24 (KJV)	17
Day 9 - Jeremiah 29: 11 (KJV)	21
Day 10 - Psalm 119: 11 (KJV)	23
Day 11 - Romans 7:23 (KJV)	27
Day 12 - Psalm 19: 7 (KJV)	29
Day 13 - Psalm 19: 14 (KJV)	31
Day 14 - Proverbs 18: 21 (KJV)	33
Day 15 - Matthew 21:22 (KJV)	37

Day 16 - Philippians 4:13 (KJV)	**41**
Day 17 - Psalms 37:23 (KJV)	**45**
Day 18 - 1 John 4:4 (KJV)	**47**
Day 19 - Psalm 139:4 (KJV)	**49**
Day 20 - Colossians 3:2 (KJV)	**51**
Day 21 - Mark 9:23 (KJV)	**55**
About the Author	**59**

Introduction

21 Day Prayer Journal

Renewing The Mind Through Daily Prayer and Affirmations

And The BIG has shown up for you and your house!

The BIG is all-powerful and possesses the divine ability to transform your mind; hence, TRANSFORMING YOUR LIFE!

A transformative mind is a renewed, positive, revived, and re-established mind.

And be not conformed to this world: but be transformed by the renewing of your mind, that you may prove what is that good and acceptable, and perfect will of God. Romans 12:1 (KJV)

You and I have something to prove, and that is the good and acceptable perfect will of God. It can only be proven when we allow the unadulterated word of God to permeate and dominate our thoughts.

When we let God's word invade our minds, we change our old thought patterns and de-construct old patterns of thinking. We adopt the mind of Christ which has no limitation. Borders merely do not exist in a renewed transformative mind!!

One can only envision what he/she could accomplish if there are no limits or fear. We could walk into the realization that all things are possible to the one that lays hold of his/her thought life. An entire world awaits you and nothing but positive energy rushes in to assist you in changing what you believe and see.

Thank you for allowing me to assist you on your journey of renewing and transforming your mind and to be a part of your Transformation Journey!

These 21 days will be a lifetime investment. This Prayer Journal along with some of my affirmations has proven to be successful in transforming the minds of many, including my own.

This is a teaching tool that is meant to help you on your journey. It serves as a blueprint including some of my favorite scriptures and my conversations with God.

My purpose for writing this journal is to help equip you with tools to aid you during your times of prayer with the Lord. It is my heartfelt prayer as you commune with Him that you can meditate and find solace in these prayers and allow the Holy Spirit to renew your mind. May you manifest all the promises of our Creator and become a powerful force to be reckoned with.

May the God of all grace and peace be with you on your 21-day journey, and may you experience His love in your life exponentially.

Love,

Mama BIG

Prophetess Patrice Jacques

Day 1:

2 Corinthians 10:3-6 (KJV) says:

- *For though we walk in the flesh, we do not war after the flesh:* The adversary is warring to high jack your thoughts.
- *For the weapons of our warfare are not carnal, but mighty through God to the pulling down of strongholds*: This part of the scripture talks about those spiritual forts that we've constructed by 'stinking thinking'; we must demolish old ways of thinking.
- *by casting down imaginations, and every high thing that exalted itself against the knowledge of God, and bringing into captivity every thought to the obedience of Christ:* We must allow God's word to be not only barometer having the last authority and say in our life. Be quick to rid your mind of evil forebodings and allow your mind to know and understand what the Spirit knows.

Prayer Affirmation: Father, I thank You that Your sweet Holy Spirit dwells in me richly. You have given me supernatural power over every enemy of my mind, and I do not have to wear my physical body out warring in the flesh. I walk in power and authority. All I must do is believe Your word and exercise my spiritual senses daily by applying the infallible word of God. It is my prayer that my thoughts are not egregious to what the bible says is my rightful inheritance. Therefore, I apply the principles of God to my life knowing that every promise is *Yay and Amen* concerning me and my family.

Reflection

Reflection

Day 2

Position yourself by giving the Holy Spirit permission to speak the truth and give your spiritual direction as you *trust in the Lord with all your heart, and lean not to your understanding: in all your way acknowledge Him, and He shall direct your paths*. Proverbs 3:5-6 (KJV)

When we modify our practices of thought toward a more focused and disciplined reflective thought life, we are better able to safeguard our minds; our thought patterns become spiritual real estate and currency that produces positive change and supernatural, manifested results.

Prayer Affirmation: Father, I give you total permission over my mind and thoughts and ask that you strengthen me to recognize the tricks and schemes of Satan. Cast down every familiar ancestral curse that tries to attach itself to my life and legacy. You are the head of my life, and I submit my ways to You daily. Help me to remain focused on you throughout my journey of renewing my mind. For I am fully persuaded that the good work that You have started you will also complete the glory and honor of our Father which is in heaven.

Reflection

Day 3

For as he thinketh in his heart, so is he.
Proverbs 23:7 (KJV)

Your mind, will, emotions, and intellect are constantly configuring your lifestyle daily. Step by step, you can engage your brain into a more directed, disciplined, and focused way of life by merely minding what you are thinking.

Prayer Affirmation: Heavenly Father, I thank You for keeping my mind in perfect peace, as I keep it on You. Today, I cooperate fully with You as You help me to make good choices and rid my mind of toxic thoughts. Today, I gather myself and ask the Holy Spirit to direct me into all truth as I focus and maintain my faith and mind on you. I commit my ways to You, Lord, knowing that you will order my steps and establish my goings. My mind is enlightened, and my pathway is clear because I follow Your voice.

Reflection

Day 4

This book of the law shall not depart out of thy mouth: but thou shall meditate therein day and night, that thou mayest observe to do according to all that is written therein: for then thou shall make thy way prosperous, and then thou shall have success.
Joshua 1:8 (KJV)

Prayer Affirmation: Today, I make a conscious effort to meditate on the word of God. I will harness my thoughts so that my mind does not wander. Thank You, Lord, that You daily load me up with benefits. I shall not want because You are my shepherd. I plant the word of God on the good soil of my heart, and it will produce a bumper crop harvest in my life. I do not allow the weeds of unforgiveness to choke my harvest. You have promised to prosper me and keep me in good health to the degree my soul prospers in you. I'm Your child. I know You love me and have provided only perfect gifts for me that only come from the Father of lights in whom there is no turning.

Reflection

Day 5:

And these words, which I command thee this day, shall be in thine heart. Deuteronomy 6:6 (KJV)

We must bind the word of God to our hearts so we do not sin against Him. To put the word in our hearts means it must be centered in our minds and first place. Renewing our minds is a daily practice, for out of your heart flows the issues of life! Your words govern what you are thinking and becoming.

Prayer Affirmation: Keep my heart pure and your word on my lips daily so that I may live the abundant life experiencing grace and favor daily! God, cause all my thoughts to become agreeable to yours and transform my thinking completely.

Reflection

Day 6

And I have said, I will bring you up and out of the affliction of Egypt unto the land of the Canaanites, and the Hittites, and the Amorites, and the Perizzites, and Hivites, and the Jebusites, unto a land flowing with milk and honey. Exodus 3: 17 (KJV)

God made a promise to his people that He was delivering them out of bondage into a place of promised blessings and favor. Egypt represents enslavement, which pales in comparison to a dwelling place flowing with provision, substance, protection, and favor.

Prayer Affirmation: I beseech You, Father, that today is the day I leave the place of slavery (thought patterns) and elevate higher in my thinking that I may possess and manifest the promises of Your provision, protection, and access overflowing favor, which is my milk and honey in Jesus's name. Selah.

Reflection

Day 7

A double-minded man is unstable in all his ways.
James 1:8 (KJV)

A double mind attracts and promotes insecurity. I am responsible for my faulty beliefs, fantasies, and insecure belief system. We must give ourselves permission to grow and act upon limiting beliefs that are merely roadblocks hindering our blessings. God is a master specialist when it comes to physical, emotional, mental, and financial healing. He wants to heal you today. Take time and be honest with Him, and He will heal you of self-doubts and doubts in God.

Prayer Affirmation: Today, I put aside my pride and become honest and transparent with You, Daddy God. Help me to not doubt your word and recognize that it is me standing in the need of prayer and a positive mind alteration. I permit You to operate on my wayward mind condition. Heal what is broken, emaciated, and fragmented in my thinking. Please help me elevate to the desired future You have ordained for me. Reinvent, a new mind and a new me as I leave behind old thoughts and become a new creation in You. No longer will I accept any vision, but the vision You have ordained for me.

Reflection

Day 8

This is the day the Lord has made; we will rejoice and be glad in it. Psalm 118:24 (KJV)

The number **eight** symbolizes **new beginnings.** What better day than today to change your thoughts and mind about yourself? We must ask ourselves this question: who is the person I will no longer allow myself to be? Change is inevitable in all our lives; change will happen either for good or bad depending on how you navigate life. God's specialty is Change! He desires that we change in our inward man so that our identity identifies with His Divinity. If you believe He is the master creator and that we are created in His image, then you must know that He will change us to live in His purpose - for HE made us and not ourselves.

Prayer Affirmation: Lord, today is Your day. I choose to be happy. I realize that Happiness is a mindset that does not depend on my external world. I bless and honor You today I trade discontentment for contentment. I refuse and disallow sadness, depression, and melodrama to live rent-free in my mind. I excavate and evict every emotional lie and replace it with love, peace, and joy. The joy of the Lord is my strength. The total of my life is choice-driven, and therefore, I choose joy and gladness. It is So and cannot be otherwise, in Jesus's name.

Reflection

Reflection

Day 9

For I know the thoughts that I think toward you, saith The Lord, thoughts of peace, and not of evil, to give you an expected end. Jeremiah 29: 11 (KJV)

Life is a journey; you and I are on our way somewhere BIG in God. We are not just meandering aimlessly, but our steps are calculated and strategic. We give the Holy Spirit authorization to lead us on our way! He is Alpha and Omega and is deserving of the names *omniscient* and *omnipresent*. He is our helper and our paraclete. He guides us with His eye. Now, let us allow that truth to penetrate our old beliefs that we are just out here by our lonesome selves trying to make things happen. Not so, that's ill thinking and must be replaced. Let us get to work on our new building (new thoughts).

Prayer Affirmation: I am your child, dear Lord. You paid the ultimate price for me by dying on the cross. You shed your precious blood to cover my sins when I was left uncovered. I'm forever grateful and align my steps with Your plans and purposes tailored and made just for me. I disavow skepticism and root criticism from my thought pattern. Today, I choose to hearken to Your voice and not follow a stranger's voice. I always bless You and rely confidently on Your word.

Reflection

_____
_____
_____
_____
_____
_____
_____
_____
_____
_____
_____
_____
_____
_____
_____
_____
_____
_____
_____
_____
_____
_____
_____
_____
_____

Day 10:

Thy word have I hid in mine heart, that I might not sin against thee. Psalm 119: 11 (KJV)

This is one of many of my favorite scriptures when it comes to renewing the mind. Behind every brain is a thinker; yes, the brain does not think! When we allow the Word to become our thinker, that in turn makes God our thinker. You may say, you cannot see the thinker. Well, have any of us seen electricity? We see the cause and effect of electricity only. In the same way, when God's word transforms our mind we cannot see Him, but we see the effects of transformation. If we cut off our hand, it ceases to hold anything in its grasp. If the eye is gouged out, we can no longer see. The word of God is our vision and our spiritual compass, even when things are dark on our path. When the scriptures are lodged in our hearts, we don't have to ever be fearful in the dark seasons of life.

Prayer Affirmation: You lead me through dark and slippery places in life. I make the sound judgment to hide Your word deep in the crevices of my heart. The heart is in the center of the human body. Even so is Your word at the center of my very being. I refuse to deviate when times get rough, not looking to none other than Jesus, my chief cornerstone. My eyes are fixed on you, as I continue looking unto the author and finisher of All that exists. Ride on King Jesus! No man can hinder Your work in my life! Ride-On!

Reflection

Reflection

Day 11

But I see another law in my members, warring against the law of my mind, and bringing me into captivity to the law of sin which is in my members. Romans 7:23 (KJV)

Who better than the apostle Paul to clearly understand the battlefield of the mind? Paul consulted the Holy Spirit three times to remove a thorn in his flesh. We may not know what his thorn was, but surely, we all can relate to sin. The good news is that we do not have to succumb to sin because the same grace that was available to the Apostle is available to each of us today!

Prayer Affirmation: Thank God for denouncing sin in the flesh finally. Sin has NO dominion over me. I step into Your grace for it is sufficient and covers all my faults and flaws. You restored my soul; my cup runs over with your goodness and tender mercies toward me. I refuse to quit, stumble, or fall under pressure. You've enlarged my steps under me, ensuring that I make it to my safe landing place. Amen

Reflection

Day 12

The law of the Lord perfect, converting the soul: the testimony of the Lord is sure, making wise the simple.
Psalm 19: 7 (KJV)

God's word washes our minds and purifies our thoughts and intentions. His word converts our minds and makes us wise even amid making problematic decisions. We can rely on and confidently trust in his cunning interventions and the craftiness of His wisdom in the affairs of humankind. He is an expert weaver and a skilled craftsman that never makes mistakes. Therefore, I trust his thoughts over the wisest of people.

Prayer Affirmation: Father of all nations, thank You in advance that I am not what I used to be nor am I who others believe me to be. Fearfully and wonderfully are the works of Your hands. You wove me in my mother's womb and allowed me to be birth at the proper season. I have been called to the kingdom for such a time as this. Have your way in my life and in my affairs. I set my affection on You because You care for me.

Reflection

Day 13

Let the words of my mouth, and the meditation of my heart, be acceptable in thy sight, Oh LORD my strength, and my redeemer. Psalm 19: 14 (KJV)

Words matter in renewing the mind! Our words are seeds that we plant in the soil of our hearts and our minds and the soil of others as well. Our words form our thoughts; our thoughts build spiritual houses in which we live. We must become the custodian of empty words and rogue thoughts, re-directing our attention from negative thinking to positive sowing. It is time to rewrite the negative narratives of our minds to become conducive to healthier thoughts.

Prayer Affirmation: Today, I make a concerted effort to quiet my mind and focus my attention on the present. I cast worries and cares of tomorrow on our Heavenly Father and dismiss the spirit of heaviness. I use my tongue as a ready writer creating a brand new world with my words. I choose to meditate on the Word and capture images in my mind of peace, prosperity, and well-being.

Reflection

Day 14

Death and life are in the power of the tongue: and they that love it shall eat the fruit thereof.
Proverbs 18: 21 (KJV)

It is time we break vicious cycles in our life. Getting control over our thoughts to break curse cycles and undo heavy burdens. One of the ways we can do this is by waging the good fight of faith through rewiring our brains. It is time for a do-over. If you realize it, we live in the world, but we do not fight as the world does. We pull down strongholds and bring those bad thoughts into captivity. We must not allow the mind to run amuck. Every thought must be evaluated and all falsehoods and arguments that are contrary to God's word must be annihilated immediately and brought into the obedience of Christ.

Prayer Affirmation: I bring every random thought that is contrary to the will and purpose of my life into the obedience of Christ. I decree that no weapon formed over my life will never work, and neither will it prosper. Every ill-spoken word said to me or about me shall fall to the ground. My life, my family, and my possessions are blessed and encompassed under the blood-stained banner. No enemy or foe can touch God's anointed. I am a friend of God; he calls me a friend. State your claim and stand your ground!

Reflection

Reflection

Day 15

And all things, whatsoever you shall ask in prayer, believing, you shall receive. Matthew 21:22 (KJV)

Prayer and faith are spiritual keys that unlock heavenly doors. When we pray, we must exercise our faith in God's word. We have to know that he cannot and will not lie. He honors His word above His name. Anything we ask in His name that coincides with HIS words he will do it!

What is Prayer? Prayer is communing with God and believing what he says will happen. My favorite saying is **believe God or believe God**!

All things are working out for my good because I love God. Things do not always feel good, but he promised me that it is working in my favor. A promise is a promise. Plainly said, any promise of God is a promise of mine, so I lay hold to His promises, which are Yay and Amen!

Prayer Affirmation: It is time to believe that THE B.I.G. DONE SHOWED UP for me! GOD, YOU ARE BIG, AND THE BIG IS GOD!! Thank You in advance for showing up and out on my behalf. I am confident that what you started in my life, you will finish. Father help me elevate to dimensions in you that I no longer limit Your word manifesting greatness and abundance on my behalf. Daddy, I ask you for the B.I.G.! You own everything! No good thing will You withhold from me, Your child. You move mountains and tell wind and rivers to peacefully be still. Show out in my life today so that men may know Your good works, and that You are real.

Reflection

Reflection

Day 16

I can do all things through Christ which strengthened me. Philippians 4:13 (KJV)

I walk in His power and might. Christ smears his Super on my natural, which allows me to do the unthinkable and achieve the unfathomable. This takes a renewed mind and a rejuvenated in Christ mindset. If I can but believe, all things are possible for me. As we continue to draw nigh to God, He comes closer to us and performs what the others may think is impossible. Even as I am typing this, I feel the urge to prophesy that you can go back to school and finish that degree! Marriages can be healed! Overcoming sickness and disease is not out of reach for the child of God!

All it takes is spending time each day in the word of God and allowing it to penetrate our thinking. Once we push out the old, distorted, mental information clouding our spiritual realms, we create a vacuum of possibilities. It is never too late to begin and, it is always too early to quit.

Prayer Affirmation: Today, I will begin again because your word is true, God. I believe that all things are possible for me. I create a new mindset of possibilities because of you, God, and my faith is taking me to a place I've never been before. Doors are opening for me; my body is healed from the crown of my head to the soles of my feet. Prosperity is my portion because you said that You give me the power to get wealth. I have only one job: believe in God! Wait on the Lord and never doubt.

Reflection

Reflection

Day 17

The steps of a good man are ordered by the Lord, and he delighted in his ways. Psalms 37:23 (KJV)

I do not have to fret because God is always near me. He delights in my ways and orders my steps into a wealthy place. As we trust Him as our source and ultimate supplier, we will always land on our feet.

Though a righteous man falls, he shall utterly rise again. Keep moving forward; you have come too far to give up now. We are not forsaken because He is a very present help to those in trouble! Can I decree that today is a day to keep walking and *Do not Die on The Step?*!

He told the children of Israel on several occasions to GO FORWARD! Go forward, child of God! Walk out of your past and move forward past hurts and disappointments; those will soon be a thing of your past. THE BIG WILL SHOW UP!

Prayer Affirmation: Father, I refuse to quit. You did not quit when it got hard so I will take advantage of the same grace You walked in when You were on the earth. Make us lie down in green pastures and restore the soul of those that are tired and perplexed. We will finish strong! We are strong in You Lord and the power of Your might.

Reflection

Day 18

Ye are of God, little children and have overcome them: because greater is He that's in you than he that is in the world. 1 John 4:4 (KJV)

That is refreshing to me to know that no power nor foes are greater than Christ. Just let that seep in for a moment! Although the world as we know it appears sometimes uncertain and chaotic, I have a bonafide promise from the Word of God - that nothing is stronger or more powerful than Elohim. When He sent Moses to tell Pharaoh to let his people go, He declared to Moses ***I AM that I AM***! Whatever you need from Him, he is the great I AM. Beloved, rest in that truth. I AM got this under control.

Prayer Affirmation: You are I AM! Because you are God, I can rest knowing that you are on my side. I AM, take the wheel of what seems to be out of control in my life and bring peace and calm. You delivered Israel with an outstretched, mighty right hand. So, Abba, stretch out in me today. Make crooked places straight and rough edges plain in the mighty name of Jeshua.

Reflection

Day 19

For there is not a word in my tongue, but lo, Oh LORD thou knowest it altogether. Psalm 139:4 (KJV)

You might ask *does God know my thoughts*? This scripture says before I utter a word He knows. I am thankful I call unto Him and He hears me. Not only does he hear but he knows my thoughts. Sometimes, we would like to hide from God, but there is nowhere we can go away from His presence. He knows our thoughts and tugs on the reins of our hearts. Intent means everything to Him! Our intentions are weighed in the balance and each of us is rewarded accordingly. Thank God He knows us holistically. Our words carry weight with Him. Renewing the mind and opening your mouth in prayer is crucial to your deliverance.

Prayer Affirmation: Lord, You know my words before I utter them. It is my prayer that the words of my mouth and the meditation of my heart be acceptable in thy sight. My God, you are my redeemer; you are my rock that provides shelter from dangers seen and unseen. You are truly my hiding place in which I find safety. Even as the deer pants for water so does my soul long after Thee. Thank You for knowing what I mean when words can't express it correctly.

Reflection

Day 20

Set your affection on things above, not on things on the earth. Colossians 3:2 (KJV)

We must practice and institute a new way of thinking when shifting our mindset into the spiritual realm. The spiritual realm is the causal realm. All things have been created for Christ and by Christ. We are seated with Him in lofty, heavenly places, where we cease fighting demons, and we become co-creators with Christ. Our words are powerful spiritual containers that fill our arenas - our minds. We are a spiritual house, a vessel where our words are the materials needed to construct our spiritual arenas. We build in the spiritual realm by using our words as collateral - building blocks that are always manifesting the B.I.G. in our lives. Good or bad, you will manifest what you speak and believe. We are seated with Christ; the seated position is resting. So, while praying I am resting and not warring.

Prayer Affirmation: Today is the day I attack my thinking and possess the mind of Christ. I am thankful that the battle has already been fought, and I have been declared a Winner! Yes, God, I bless You because I always win; you have won for all of us on the cross.

God, You fought every spiritual battle so I may sit with you. Today, I elevate my low-level vibrations and mount up on eagles' wings. I trade my imperfect thinking for a more perfect train of thought. Today is a new day, and I will think and see myself as Christ sees me. I am created in His image. I can and will see myself as an overcomer in Jesus's name. Yay and Amen!

Reflection

Reflection

Day 21

Jesus said unto him, If thou canst believe, all things are possible to him that believeth. Mark 9:23 (KJV)

This is scripture is loaded with possibilities! **All** merely means ALL. All is inclusive of everything and exclusive of nothing. Hear Him speaking to you. God cannot and will not lie; if He spoke it, he makes it good. We are possessors, just as he spoke to Abraham in the book of Genesis. God made a covenant with Abraham and said he would be a possessor of both heaven and earth. That same promise is available to the child of God today.

It is time to be transformed by the renewing of our minds so we can live our best lives! The price has been paid; your tickets have been punched. It is my prayer that we step into the river, and do not get stuck on the steps of life.

Child of God, it is our time and our season. All things are freely ours and are just waiting for you and me to manifest the promises of God in our personal lives. All we have to do is make the choice, keep the faith, change our mindset, and believe!

Prayer Affirmation: I am a child of the Most High God,

and my life will never be the same. For today, I apply pressure to my life and accept the challenge of renewing my mind and minding my words. I will put in the necessary work that it takes to change my limited thinking into unlimited possibilities. The blessings of the Lord are upon my life, and I have the mind of Christ!

Reflection

Reflection

About the Author

Patrice S Jacques

Patrice Jacques, also affectionately known as "Mama BIG!" She loves God more than anything and live her life pleasing to her heavenly father.

Patrice is a sought-after empowerment masterclass specialist, her gifting and anointing as a Prophet is revolutionary. She's an educator and a thinker, and a transformational leader to many. She's a life coach and pusher for many leaders in the body of Christ! Her distinguishing reputation as change agent has earned her the title "Mama BIG", based on the profound revelation given to her by God, called THE BIG!!

She's the mother, of four beautiful children, JaJuan, Zachary, Dana, and Rachael. She absolutely adores her Grannies and great grands.

Patrice, is a sought after Preacher and teacher in the body of Christ. She walks in a heavy Prophetic anointing and a sure word of Prophecy in her mouth. Many lives have been changed through her ministry.

She's an author of "THE BIG DONE SHOWED UP!"

She holds a Master's Degree from Loyola University. However, her work in the classroom as educator is fulfilling, but pales in comparison to the mandate and assignment as one of Gods Change Agents.

To connect with Prophetess Jacques, follow her on social media below:

FB @patricejacques

IG @ladyprophetubettaknowit

Clubhouse @thebigroom

Email her at Thebigdoneshowedup@gmail.com

www.ingramcontent.com/pod-product-compliance
Lightning Source LLC
Chambersburg PA
CBHW080456170426
43196CB00016B/2829